John XXIII

A Saint for the Modern World

LUCINDA M. VARDEY
Afterword by Yves Congar

Paulist Press
New York / Mahwah, NJ

Novalis
Toronto, Canada

Cover image copyright © Bettmann/CORBIS. Used with permission.
Cover and book design by Lynn Else

Originally printed in *Traveling with the Saints in Italy*, published by Hidden-Spring, an Imprint of Paulist Press, copyright © 2005 by Lucinda Vardey. New content and revisions contained herein include the Introduction, The Legacy, and some essential updates throughout the text.

Library of Congress Cataloging-in-Publication Data
Vardey, Lucinda.
    John XXIII : a saint for the modern world / Lucinda M. Vardey, afterword by Yves Congar.
        pages cm
    Includes bibliographical references.
    ISBN 978-0-8091-4891-2 (alk. paper)
    1. John XXIII, Pope, 1881–1963. 2. John XXIII, Pope, 1881–1963—Influence. 3. Popes—Biography. I. Title.
    BX1378.2.V37 2014
    282.092—dc23
    [B]   2013051028

Published in Canada by Novalis
Publishing Office
10 Lower Spadina Ave., Suite 400
Toronto, Ontario, Canada
M5V2Z2

Published by Paulist Press
997 Macarthur Boulevard
Mahwah, New Jersey 07430

www.paulistpress.com

Head Office
4475 Frontenac St.
Montréal, Québec, Canada
H2H 2S2

www.novalis.ca

ISBN: 978-2-89688-014-0 (pbk.)

Printed and bound in the
United States of America

Library and Archives Canada Cataloguing
in Publication:
BX1378.2.V37 2014 282.092 C2013-908514-9

CONTENTS

To the Most Reverend Joseph W. Tobin C.Ss.R.

INTRODUCTION

I n John XXIII's hometown in northern Italy, where votives are hung in various places in gratitude for his intercession, the most common of prayers answered is for fertility. Couples unable to conceive have petitioned the man who taught the primacy of human life, who promoted the vital centrality of family, who loved children—and their prayers have been heard. This pope extended his embrace not only to all families, but to the largest family in the world—the entire human race.

John XXIII's papacy began in 1958 when the whole world was changing dramatically. In the aftermath of two world wars, humanity was still particularly vulnerable. There was widespread precariousness, due partly to an enduring nuclear threat brought to a head in the Cold War, an obsessive nervousness about the popular spread of communism in the West, and the shared trauma of Jewish people who had survived the Holocaust. For the first time, many countries under foreign rule were vying for independence, while colonial superpowers were forced to cede their control of peoples of different cultures and beliefs. Workers were finding a collective voice on fair labor, income, and safety; and women were expressing their rights to be heard and treated equally. Science was making extraordinary leaps by readying a man to walk on the moon and providing us with a picture of the fragile beauty of planet earth. The age of technology was accelerating and with it the beginning surge toward globalization.

Pope John entered his papacy at the age of seventy-seven with an already rich experience of life formed by living and working in a variety of diverse cultures, religions, and peoples. He brought with him a practical knowledge of poverty and riches, of ministering in wars and in peace. This knowledge proved to be invaluable, as he was propelled into a leadership role for not only the Church but the secular world. He knew that the Church could not be kept separate from the workings of the world. He strongly believed that spiritual values needed to be exerted as the "guiding influence" on all "components" such as culture, social institutions, economics, politics, law, and science—all that made up "the external community" of humanity and "its continual development" (*Pacem in Terris* 36). Above all, John XXIII upheld the pursuit of truth and freedom as basic needs for both men and women: that each person should be free to seek truth and meaning as a right in itself.

He promoted the dignity of employment, and the essentiality of care and stability for the aged, disabled, and those suffering loss. He became an essential pivot for balancing the spiritual with the secular: of not losing sight of one by focusing solely on the other. That was his greatest legacy. He could read the "signs of the times." In five short years, he managed to change what seemed to be unchangeable: not only minds and dogmatic rigidities but also the hearts and souls of individual people. He opened everyone to the transformative relevance and vitality of the gospel and, by providing an alternative to the prevailing attitudes of entrenchment, he created the conditions for hope.

John XXIII's story is one of heroic proportions: he not only reshaped single-handedly the role and activities of the papacy and the institutional Catholic Church, but his thirst for unity and peace introduced the atmosphere for dialogue as an alternative to defense. He reminded us that there is a better way to steer the course of history and "prepare a glorious future" (*Journal of a Soul*). We have to do it together, he said. And we have to do it with God.

HIS LIFE

This is a story of a man from a humble background who, through the force of his faith and reliance on God's will, became first a priest, then bishop, Vatican envoy and nuncio, cardinal, and finally pope. It is also a heroic story of a soul who was born into a farming family in a village outside Bergamo in northern Italy. Having learned to read and write, he kept a diary for sixty-seven years, which charted the intimate details of the joys, challenges, and struggles of his soul's growth. Because of this diary, and his generosity at willing it for publication after his death (to enable it to help people, he had said), he has opened up the course of his interior mystical life, spiritual purification, enlightenment, and final unity with God. One of his biographers, Peter Hebblethwaite, wrote that the end of the diary (now a book called *Journal of a Soul*) "crowns and explains the beginning."

This is also a story about a traditional priest who longed for simple service and chastised himself for his personal imperfections, who journeyed to faraway and exotic places to minister to those of diverse faiths, learning language upon language to be able to understand and serve the people, never knowing the reason until the end of his life. It is a miraculous story of how a soul thirsting for perfection, who began life "under the mountain" (the name of his village being *Sotto Il Monte*), pulled himself and all Christians up a spiritual mountain to view their lives of faith from a higher and different perspective. After three years of preparation for the Second Vatican Council, Pope John XXIII wrote that "we are now on the slopes of the sacred mountain." He reached the pinnacle by embracing the world like a great-grandfather, making everyone feel part of one family. But there is far more to "Good Pope John."

Angelo Giuseppe Roncalli was born on November 25, 1881, in his parents' bed in a peasant hamlet in Sotto Il Monte, a village of about twelve hundred inhabitants. His birth was cause for much rejoicing in the Roncalli household. His father, Giovanni, and his mother, Maria, were delighted to have a son, a brother for his three sisters, and a future helper on the land. As was the custom, he was baptized the same day at the local church. Called Santa Maria di Brusicco, it was about a hundred yards from the Roncalli home. His godfather was the patriarch of the Roncalli clan, Zio Zaverio—although he was only his great-uncle, being his deceased grandfather's brother. Zaverio was pious and well-read, and, without children of his own, took it on himself to become a second father to Angelo. In his diary, Angelo wrote, "Hardly had that good old man, my uncle Zaverio, presented me, a newborn babe, at the baptismal font, than he consecrated me there in the little church of my own village to the Sacred Heart, so that I should grow up under its protection, a good Christian."

The significance of his given names—and later the name he chose as pope—was always foremost in his mind. Angelo, meaning "angel," was a compelling challenge; he once remarked that he felt under an obligation to always behave like one, when he knew, on the contrary, that he was "no angel at all." His second name, Giuseppe, meaning Joseph, was in honor of "the dear Patriarch" of the family of Jesus, and St. Joseph became his spiritual protector.

Angelo's earliest memory was when he was four years old. It was on the Feast of Mary's Presentation in the Temple, November 1885. His pregnant mother had dragged all her young children on a short pilgrimage to the shrine of Madonna delle Caneve on the edge of the surrounding woods. When they arrived, the chapel was already full so they had to stand outside. Angelo remembered being lifted up by his mother so that he could see through the small window, and she said to him, "Look, Angelino, look how beautiful the Madonna is. I have consecrated you wholly to her."

Life for the Roncallis was not easy. Like most peasant families, they were professional sharecroppers, which meant that half the land's produce was shared with their landlords and the rest kept for feeding a family of up to twenty people at a time. Angelo remembered that his parents would also invite hungry strangers home, so there would sometimes be less food for the children. There was never bread on the table, only *polenta* (cornmeal), and he had only one pair of shoes to last all his childhood.

Angelo spent more time in church as an altar boy than he did in the village school, although he was the brightest pupil. Nurturing his young nephew's devotion and vocation, Uncle Zaverio arranged for Angelo to take Latin lessons with a priest from the next village. Although Angelo recalled it as a harrowing experience with beatings for grammatical errors, he came to passionately love Latin.

The local parish priest, who resided in Angelo's baptismal church, was Don Francesco Rebuzzini, a model of holiness exemplifying the perfect priest to young Angelo. What he noticed in Rebuzzini's ministry, which would become a teaching he would later cherish, was that he practiced holiness in virtual obscurity. Angelo called his parish priest "the saintly guardian of my childhood and vocation" because, after Angelo declared his intentions for the priesthood, Don Francesco prepared him for the entrance exams to the seminary in nearby Bergamo. Later, when Angelo came home for the holidays, he was about to serve at Mass when Don Francesco dropped dead in the sacristy. Angelo recalled it as the first great tragedy of his life; he wrote how heartbroken he was, and how looking at the seventy-three-year-old priest's body on the floor reminded him of a statue of the dead Jesus. Don Francesco had bequeathed his personal copy of the *Imitation of Christ* to Angelo, which he treasured all his life.

Bergamo was a bustling city that had been under Venetian rule for over three hundred years. At the time Angelo entered the junior seminary at the age of ten, it was undergoing modernization with railway links to nearby Milan and Brescia, and with a growing industry in textile manufacturing. Angelo loved the city and embraced its historic and spiritual culture with vigor, but even more important for him was its link with St. Charles Borromeo, the sixteenth-century archbishop of Milan and founder of his seminary. Recognized by the Council of Trent as a "model bishop," Borromeo became an example for the young seminarian to follow. Angelo wrote in his diary that he would "try to make this great saint more and more familiar to my heart and mind, to pray to him frequently for his help and to imitate him." In fact, Angelo always felt called to imitate not only Borromeo but also other saints especially close to him. Among these were Francis de Sales, patron of writers and journalists; John Berchmans; Gregory Babarigo, who reformed the seminary after Borromeo and whom Angelo, when pope, canonized; Philip Neri; Ignatius of Loyola, founder of the Jesuits; and Catherine of Siena. Angelo often chided himself for not being more like them when they were his age. Yet, the lives and examples of the many saints he loved became, in fact, the link to holiness that he had witnessed from his parish priest. He was beginning to put together a composite of what holiness was, what himself was perhaps striving for. Two of the most vital teachings that emerged from his diary were that holiness is not dependent on the sensational but on "little things which seem but trifles in the eyes of the world," and that saints, especially in their youth, looked as if they were taking a quite different route than the one in which their "natural gifts and brilliant qualities had seemed to indicate." He noticed that their practice of "holy detachment" allowed them to be able to hear God's voice, the way that he could hear God speaking to him. He also indirectly admonished himself by claiming that there was no cause for pride in anything the saints succeeded in doing while they worked at reforming and founding orders, healing and transforming the world. All they did, he wrote, was to "cast themselves blindly into all that God wanted them to do."

THE WAY OF PERFECTION

In the senior seminary in Bergamo, Angelo began to set out on a series of disciplines for the deepening of his interior life. His spiritual aim was "at perfection," and his course became one of daily obstacles and struggles with his humanity. He wrote that although he aimed at perfection in practice, he was far from succeeding; in learning surrender, he knew that it was not to be mapped out by him but by God. However, he also knew that he needed a spiritual discipline to tame him and keep him on his course, and he advised himself to be careful not to get sidetracked by thoughts and activities that would take him away from his "pursuit of the interior life. Every stray thought that enters my mind breaks off a bit of my inner self," he wrote. He faced the challenge of duality that battled inside him for dominance—which he viewed as a battle of interior good and evil—and he would catch himself on the vice of pride, writing that if he continued with his captive pride prominent in all that he said and did, then "in the end, what shall I be?—a windbag!" He had to convince himself of what he called "the great truth," which was that "Jesus wants me, the seminarist Angelo Roncalli, not just a mediocre but a supreme virtue; he will not be satisfied with me until I have made myself, or at least have done my utmost to make myself holy. The graces he has given me to this end are so many, and so great." He listed the gifts and graces he had received so far—that he, "a country lad... with the affection of a loving mother," was taken from his home and given all that he needed. He was hungry and Christ fed him, had nothing to wear and Christ clothed him, had no books to carry to his studies and Christ provided those also. He recalled that many times he forgot Christ but that Christ never forgot him, and "gently recalled me. If my affection for him cooled, he warmed me in his breast, at the flame with which his heart is always burning." These early expressions of the motherhood of Christ contributed to his model of behavior as a future pastor.

Part of the challenge of growing up, growing away, and practicing "holy detachment" was his changing relationship with his mother. He had been very close to her as a child, but on one vacation visit home from the seminary, he felt ostracized by the family. This was largely due to their mis-understanding of his call to the priesthood. Some family members viewed his departing for Bergamo as an irresponsible desire to avoid farm work. Sitting in the parlor study-ing during the summer didn't make sense to them. In addition, his mother, feeling his emotional distance, accused him of not liking her, which upset him tremen-dously. In order to cheer him up, the local priest (the suc-cessor to Don Francesco) gave Angelo a trip to Rome to celebrate Pope Leo XIII's ninetieth year, along with a short pilgrimage to Assisi and Loreto. On his return to Bergamo, Angelo reached out to his mother in a letter of prophetic consolation: "Even if I was pope, you would always remain for me the greatest lady in the world."

A SPIRITUAL QUEST

In 1900, at the age of nineteen, Angelo took the overnight train from Bergamo to Rome to take an exam for a theology scholarship. He wrote of his love of the pomp and pageantry of the Vatican. Receiving a blessing from the pope at St. Peter's, he also received an award for Hebrew and he excelled in his exams. His studies were interrupted, however, in November 1901 when he was called to compulsory military service in the Lombardy Brigade in Bergamo, which he called his "year of Babylonian captivity." His time in the military also tested his way of perfection. It was far from a perfect environment for a twenty-year-old seminarian. He wrote of the locker-room ambience, of rough language and blatant sexuality, and he prided himself more for remaining "unpolluted" than for being promoted from corporal to sergeant. Fearful that he might lose his vocation, he found that it was strengthened even more by his year in the military, and he felt restless to continue his studies and to familiarize himself "with the scientific moment in all its manifestations."

He saw his move to Rome as a gift from the motherly care of God; that God through "countless acts of kindness," had brought him to the headquarters of his Church. He mused that it must be for a purpose that he was there, and that even if he were made pope in the future (with all its fame and prestige), he would still have to stand for divine judgment at the end of his life, and be asked the question, "What should I be worth then?" His personal and spiritual scrutiny continued in earnest as, at the age of twenty-one, he became a subdeacon, which was prior to final vows, at a solemn ceremony at St. John Lateran. He felt a newness in himself, a sense of moving forward, as he took the sacramental steps toward the priesthood.

His doctorate in theology then in preparation (and supervised by Eugenio Pacelli, who was the future Pope Pius XII), Don Roncalli was ordained in 1904 at the Church of Santa Maria in the Piazza del Popolo in Rome. Almost as a reminder of his mother's early consecration of her son to the Madonna, he said that at the altar, when he was swearing his eternal fidelity to his superior bishop, he looked up above the tabernacle at the "blessed image of Our Lady" who he had not noticed before, and she seemed to be smiling down at him. He felt a "sweet peace" in his soul and "a generous and confident spirit," and he heard her tell him she would watch over him and was pleased with his ordination. His first Mass was said, aptly, in the crypt at St. Peter's Basilica, and one of his professors had arranged for him to have an audience and blessing with Pope Pius X. He knelt at the feet of a man whom he had followed as a cardinal, who had been patriarch of Venice, and the first pope from peasant stock.

Don Roncalli's first assignment as priest was secretary to the newly appointed bishop of Bergamo, Msgr. Radini Tedeschi. He also became professor in the seminary at which he had been a student.

PRIESTHOOD

As a newly ordained priest, Don Roncalli took his duties seriously and his soul growth continued under meticulous scrutiny. He experienced "indescribable joys" and gratitude for the many graces he was receiving and feeling, although he made sure to add that he was a most unworthy recipient. He continued to monitor his pride, his unnecessary conversations; even his natural ability for leadership and teaching was not something to celebrate. He confronted himself on various incidences where he was not following his way of perfection, and wrote prayers pleading for heavenly intercession for his errors. He expected himself to be an example of a good "priestly character" in his gestures, speech, and dress (as it was defined by the Council of Trent). He noted that Jesus Christ during the first thirty years of his life "offered me a whole series of shining examples," to which he added the scriptural quote from Exodus 25:40: "See that you make them according to the pattern."

His bishop was a man he admired and respected, who took the place of his first parish priest, Don Francesco, as mentor, advisor, and example, and Don Roncalli served him loyally and efficiently until the end of Tedeschi's life. They traveled together to the Holy Land in 1905, as well as to the original Benedictine monastery at Subiaco, south of Rome. Tedeschi guided his secretary through many of the challenges prompted by secular life in Italy at the time, particularly what was referred to as "the social question," which caused the Church to respond to the emerging changes between civic and ecclesiastical life. This also provided the seedbed for Roncalli's future ministry of opening the Church to the world. In the meantime, the keen professor loved his seminarian students, wanting to be able to teach them in humility and prayer.

OUTBREAK OF WAR

During the outbreak of World War I in August 1914, after Pope Pius X had died, perhaps of a broken heart, Don Roncalli's Bishop Tedeschi also passed away, his last words being "for peace, for peace."

Don Roncalli began his war ministry as a medical orderly and later an army chaplain at the Bergamo hospital. He remembered this time as one of long vigils among the bunks of brave soldiers, receiving their confessions, preparing them for death. He remembered the hymns to Mary that "rose up around simple, improvised altars," Masses in the fields, sacrifices of families, losses, and grief. Demobilized in December 1918, the young priest promptly destroyed his uniform. But this time in the army had been different from his military service as a seminarian. This time he had been able to bring the principles he had been working so hard to achieve in himself into action for service to others.

The new pope in Rome was Benedict XV, who was a political "neutralist" like Don Roncalli, and, as soon as he was out of his military uniform, Roncalli was appointed spiritual director of the seminary. He founded the student's hostel, which he called "the darling of my heart," installing a huge mirror in its hall with the words "Know Thyself" over it. He began lecturing there on topics that showed his own intellectual interests: "The Church, Science, and the School," "Christianity and Greco-Roman Science," "Astrology, Alchemy, and the Intellectual Aberrations of the Middle Ages," "The University and Scholasticism," "The Church and the Renaissance," and "Modern Struggles for Freedom in Education." He also lectured on St. Catherine of Siena to the National Union of Catholic Women, to which he was serving as chaplain.

A PILGRIM IN ROME

Don Roncalli had written in his journal after a visit to Rome that he didn't like the Roman atmosphere, that he felt only like a pilgrim in Rome, and that, even though there was always good to be done everywhere, he wouldn't want to live there. He had been working through his interior journey dealing with his imaginings of what lay ahead for him, and then scolding himself for not living according to Divine Providence and doing God's will in the moment. Just as if he was ready for the next stage in his inner life, which was to practice obedience without question, he was appointed to work with the Roman curia in the Vatican in the distinguished Congregation for the Propagation of Faith. In 1921, despite his desire to never live in Rome, he arrived there with his belongings, turning down a seven-room apartment for something cheaper, and inviting his sisters Ancilla and Maria to become his housekeepers. He stayed for four years.

A "PROLONGED MISSION" IN BULGARIA

Don Angelo Roncalli must have proved himself during his time working at the Vatican, although he frequently wondered where God would put him next. His appointment by the new pope, Pius XI, to become apostolic visitor in Sofia, Bulgaria, was certainly a surprise. It was 1925, and Don Angelo was in his mid-forties. A promotion came with the job, and before leaving he was consecrated bishop on March 19, the feast of one of his namesakes, St. Joseph; what's more, it took place in San Carlo al Corso, a church in Rome dedicated to another one of his patrons, St. Charles Borromeo, who was also the subject of Roncalli's labors on what was to become a five-volume edition of Borromeo's writings and teachings. Members of the Roncalli family from Sotto Il Monte came to Rome for this special occasion. A photograph taken at the time shows a stout man who seems naturally suited to the vestige of bishopric. He had written in his diary that bishop's robes are a reminder of the "splendor of souls," which they signified, and that this was the bishop's "real glory." He now had to assume new aspects in himself—*digne, attente, devote* (with dignity, attentiveness, and devotion), which he needed to express in his work and solely "for the edification of souls." He advised himself to do "ordinary things day after day, without over-anxiety, without ostentation" and to carry these out with "fervor and perfection." His way of perfection was still unfolding, but another thing that needed his attention was his physical weight. He disliked exercise so he had to find a way to curb his appetite and his "greedy palate." He set out diets for himself, cutting down his food portions, watering down his wine, but his attempts at losing weight seemed hopeless. Perhaps he was promising too much to God and himself about dieting. He hadn't the discipline because he liked to dine, and he relished building community by eating together at table like one large family. He accepted his destiny as being "fat and heavy," and later, when elected pope, the Vatican tailor had to hold together the largest cassock in the papal wardrobe with safety pins so that the new Pope John XXIII could appear in the appropriate garb on the balcony at St. Peter's.

He was by then old and disinterested enough to make jokes about his physical appearance, which he did frequently. Once he said that, when he felt too fat, he would go and stand next to Cardinal Cicognani (the stoutest man in the curia), which then made him feel as "thin as a rail!"

The post as bishop in Bulgaria was to prove invaluable in his later ministry, although he admitted that the "prolonged mission" of his ten monotonous years there caused him "acute and intimate suffering," which he tried not to show. His lonely isolation from friends and family combined with the many trials he endured representing the papacy in a country where the Orthodox Church was the prominent religion. He was, of course, sowing seeds in a ground that had hardened to the concepts of reconciliation and dialogue. He befriended Orthodox Church leaders, among them the Armenian patriarch, who later asked to die with a papal medal that Bishop Roncalli had given him placed upon his heart. There were small signs of hope between the various religions, as Roncalli set about to be "good and kind," to persevere with patience, to represent the pope and the Roman Catholic Church, and to "exercise pastoral and fatherly kindness, such as befits a shepherd and father," which he defined as his "whole purpose of my life as Bishop." Ultimately he came to love the Bulgarians and learned of the importance of understanding a people and the history of a place. He became able to adequately explain to others the philosophy of the historic, not only of the past but also of the present, "even the history that is now before our eyes."

What Angelo Roncalli was creating was a widening path through the world. Still checking in on his interior motives—of the need to be moderate in speech, tranquil in thoughts, loving and caring, open and embracing—he was learning the elements of spiritual and secular precepts in his own particular style and way, which would benefit him greatly in what lay ahead.

BUILDING BRIDGES THROUGH DIPLOMACY

In 1935, Bishop Roncalli was posted as Vatican envoy to Turkey and Greece. He arrived in historic Istanbul (previously Constantinople) to face the challenges of unity among the Christian Churches in a prominent Islamic country, which disallowed the wearing of clerical vestments. As a man who favored robes of dignity, he accepted civilian wear as an opportunity to practice priestly attributes and virtues without the external trappings, although he didn't find it easy. The experience, however, might have enabled him to more fully understand and sympathize with the role of the laity, those followers of God who attempt to practice Christ's teachings in ordinary life. But this was not ordinary life, because ill winds were blowing through Europe that would eventually lead to the outbreak of another world war. In Rome, Pius XI passed away, and one of Bishop Roncalli's former theology professors, Eugenio Pacelli, was elected Pope Pius XII. It is reported that Roncalli said, "Being pope today is enough to turn your hair as white as your soutane" (the papal cassock).

Matters back in Rome made things difficult for Roncalli; he alluded to the toughness of dealing with the curia on affairs of diplomacy as well as ecumenism. He began to learn Turkish and would introduce Turkish words into the liturgy (an early sign of what was to come in liturgical and vernacular reform at Vatican II). While in Turkey he never wanted to visit Greece, and once he got there, he always felt "like a fish in water." During the late thirties, he was viewed with suspicion in Greece, especially when Italian troops were posted at its borders prior to their North African defeat, but he stepped in to help trace prisoners of war with the Red Cross, as the Vatican became central to gaining information on the whereabouts of prisoners of war from all sides of the fighting. While the Holy See remained silent about the persecution of Jews, Bishop Roncalli offered as much practical help as he could. With the aid of King Boris of Bulgaria, whom he had befriended when he lived in Sofia, he gained transit visas to Palestine for many Jewish people who were vulnerable to being sent to concentration camps. The chief rabbi of Jerusalem, Isaac Hertzog, wrote to Roncalli expressing his gratitude "for the energetic steps that you have taken and will undertake to save our unfortunate people, innocent victims of unheard of horrors, [and I acknowledge the] noble feelings of your own heart."

At a peace service he led in Istanbul's cathedral, Bishop Roncalli offered a concluding prayer for unity, citing that whatever race we are, whatever religion we belong to, or whatever tradition or social position we have, we are in the end all members of the same human family. It was the crowning statement of his appointment, one that was to be his primary link to the desires he knew of Christ for the unity of the world. He said of war that it is instigated by the "prince of this world," who has nothing to do with Christ, who is "the Prince of Peace." And then, as if forecasting hope and healing, he announced in 1944 that the Holy Spirit may seem lost to the world, but was still at work— "mysteriously and powerfully"—within it.

THE ONLY MAN IN PARIS...

Much to his—and everyone else's surprise—Bishop Roncalli was made papal nuncio to France, an appointment announced soon after Pius XII's meeting with General De Gaulle and the liberation of Paris to the Allied armies in August 1944. In December Roncalli arrived in a divided Catholic France, due to the aftermath of the Resistance movement. However, there were other divisions, the most prominent created by members of the clerical hierarchy who didn't know him at all. He was perceived to have been shunted off to the Balkans for twenty years, which were a "backwater" to France and not part of the central diplomatic scene, and at sixty-three he was considered, according to one prelate, "an old fogy." Yet this prestigious diplomatic post, probably one of the highest accorded by the Vatican, did not intimidate the new nuncio. He was more than well prepared: for most of his adult life, he had been working on his way of perfection; it was clear, simple, and directive. And, with his caution for not being inwardly distracted by the ways of the world, he could offer the world something different, something intimate.

From the start, everything Roncalli did was considered right. He wrote to all the bishops of the Church of France in a friendly and open manner, respecting everyone's opinion, and treating them with openness and kindness. He took to decorating his diplomatic apartments—something he said was important for the work he had to do. He became a familiar figure in the streets, walking around his quarter of Paris, even though Pope Pius XII suggested that it was undignified for a nuncio to do so. He began learning French, meeting and speaking with as many people as wanted to see him, and he said, "A good table and a good cellar are great assets." He also gained a reputation for being a brilliant conversationalist, a master of diplomacy who weighed his words carefully. One Venetian commented that his "graceful conversation was like lacework or subtle embroidery." After Roncalli hired a chef who later became the proprietor of the reputable restaurant La Grenoville, his dinners were considered the best on the circuit. But more than that, he gained a reputation as a man who was imbued with the grace of God. Author Robert Schuman said of him that he was the only man in Paris in "whose company one feels a physical sensation of peace."

France provided the ground for further education for Roncalli. Although he was careful to walk what seemed to be a conservative and conventional line in his work as nuncio, his eyes didn't miss the "signs of the times," a term he adopted as pope from the then-banned French theologian

Chenu. Social changes were in the air as the priest-worker movement was expanding and challenging the Church to look seriously at social action, equality, and justice as central to the work of Christ. Roncalli took up reading Simone Weil, the Jewish/Christian French writer and activist, and he began introducing ground rules of dialogue to the Catholic members of UNESCO; he also continued his work on the writings and teachings of St. Charles Borromeo.

It was ten years before he was called back home to his beloved Italy, closer to his blood family, who had visited him frequently, his brothers astonished at having been whisked around the great European city in a black Cadillac.

As he prepared to leave Paris, Roncalli was visited by many dignitaries to say good-bye and wish him well. The Canadian ambassador, Georges Vanier, told him that he had three of the characteristic products of Bergamo—wine, silk, and steel—wine representing his warmth of heart and vivacity of spirit, silk for his "sense of nuances," and steel for the firmness of his character, which "makes no compromise where truth is concerned."

A SHEPHERD AND FATHER

Throughout Roncalli's career, he had heard rumors about the greater things that were in store for his future, although he attempted to make a joke of them, seeing them as an opportunity to further his interior detachment from expectations of honors and promotions. He also wished to perfect the same virtue in cases of humiliation or opposition, and had begun to feel the fruit of his interior labor when he wrote in his diary, "Nothing of all this causes me any anxiety or preoccupation." As if to gauge how he was doing with his practice of detachment, his next appointment was, naturally, to the college of cardinals in 1953, along with the added prestigious position of patriarch of Venice three months later. He was at last to return to his native soil, and to the Veneto region of the north so near his Bergamese home. "It is he [the Lord] who has really done all, and done it without my help, for I could never have imagined or desired such greatness," he wrote in his diary. He saw this appointment like an arc beginning in his native village and curving over "the domes and pinnacles of St. Mark's" (the great church in the main piazza of Venice). At the same time, he received sad news from home. His beloved sister Ancilla, whom he called "the most precious treasure of my household," died of stomach cancer. In his absence abroad, he had rented part of a house called Casa Martino in his hometown to spend a month each year during his vacation. His unmarried sisters lived—and died—in that apartment, which he wanted them to have as a home especially after their parents had passed away.

Roncalli viewed his purpose as cardinal as a sacred mission: "To save souls and guide them to heaven." He was happy—and possibly relieved—to be out of official diplomacy and back to where he began as a young priest, a pastor and shepherd to his Venetian flock.

As someone who favored ceremony, he kept the tradition of entering Venice in a procession of gondolas and cut a fine figure as the people lined the canals and streets to greet him. Following in the footsteps of Pius X, he moved into the Episcopal Palace near St. Mark's overlooking the Piazzetta Dei Leoncini, choosing the second rather than the first floor as his residence. He provided an open door policy to all and put a sign over his study that read "Shepherd and Father." He also referred to himself as mother "of a poor family who is entrusted with so many children," as his time was stretched with endless requests for meetings, help, care, sacraments, and other calls for ministry. One of his first appointments, which he had to defend for breaking tradition, was of Don Loris Capovilla as his secretary. Capovilla, like Roncalli himself, was from a poor background instead of the traditional nobility, and came from the Padua diocese with experience as a journalist. Peter Hebblethwaite, in his biography of Pope John XXIII, wrote, "In Capovilla, Roncalli got much more than a secretary: he got a spiritual son, a literary executor, a confidante, and a Boswell."

During his five years in Venice, Cardinal Roncalli witnessed and celebrated the canonization of Pius X (whom he honored by giving communion to Pius X's grandnephews and nieces), and he continued his ecumenical work by regularly meeting with leaders of other churches, including the Melkite patriarch Maximos IV Saigh, whom he later invited to the Vatican Council. Roncalli noted, maybe for the first time by the official Church, that Catholics cannot blame—and accuse—solely the Protestant and Orthodox Christian Churches for the split with Rome, but need to take some responsibility themselves for possibly prompting the split by the actions, or inactions, of the Holy See. So as to prove his point, he opposed the official papal consecration of the Feast of the Queenship of Mary, which he saw as an obstacle to ecumenical dialogue. All the while, he continued to reach out to those he considered opponents, "if not enemies," and provided a basis for cooperation between the Church and the political parties of the left. The themes of his lectures also illustrated his ministry and reflected his pastoral experience: "The Church in the Slav World," "The Church and Separated Oriental Christians," "The Church and Protestant Confessions." Now that he was in Italy, he didn't forget the people he had served in other parts of the world. He wrote that he remembered France, Turkey, Greece, and Bulgaria in his daily prayers.

The fact that, at his age, he was probably nearing the end of his life was a truth he wanted to ignore. "My mind resents this and almost rebels," he wrote, because on good days he still felt young, "agile and alert." But he admitted that he was feeling "on the threshold of eternity" as he prepared his last will.

A SPIRIT OF CHANGE

Cardinal Roncalli had always been interested in the papacy. His love of history and the Church motivated his study, and he knew much more about the popes of the past than most of his contemporaries. Summoned to Rome in October 1958 after the death of Pope Pius XII, he and the other cardinals arrived for the conclave. Kneeling in the crypt of St. Peter's (a place so close to his heart from the first Mass he had said there as a young priest), Roncalli prayed to St. Peter to protect and guide the conclave. Almost immediately, he was among the favored—one cardinal exclaimed that he could imagine kneeling at his feet. During the conclave, Cardinal Roncalli wrote to the then-bishop of Bergamo, exclaiming that his soul had found comfort and confidence "that a new Pentecost can blow through the Church, renewing its head, leading to a new ordering of the ecclesiastical body, and bringing fresh vigor in progress toward the victory of truth, goodness, and peace." He was hopeful that the new pope would be a part of this divine plan, and became delighted when his popularity seemed to be diminishing during the early rounds of voting. But the cardinals had agreed that they needed a man with spiritual strength and charity, one who belonged to all peoples—especially the poor and those under totalitarian persecution—someone who could exemplify the subtle art of diplomacy, who could comfort the doubters, who could listen, encourage, and bring hope. No one fit the bill more perfectly than Cardinal Roncalli.

When he was elected by thirty-eight votes, with heavy support from the French delegates, he wrote in his diary at the end of the day, "I'm ready." He prayed to the saints, particularly St. Pius X, for "calmness and courage." He chose the name John—not Pius or Leo or Benedict, as expected. There was a spirit of change in the air, and his choice of name was another sign. He explained that he chose John because of St. John Lateran (the official church of the bishop of Rome, a promotion he had just assumed), and it was also the name of the fourth evangelist, one who had so beautifully recorded Christ's teachings of unity and oneness and of the final message, "Love one another as I have loved you." It was because of John the Baptist as well, not only the great biblical prophet but also the name of Roncalli's own father, Giovanni Battista. And it was the name of a tower on top of the mountain behind Sotto Il Monte, which he loved and recalled as part of the joys of his childhood. Last, but not least, with his knowledge of the troubled succession of all the Pope Johns (particularly the last, an antipope in 1410 by the name of Baldassar Cossa, who took the name Pope John XXIII), Roncalli wiped him out in the apostolic succession by assuming the same name. He announced that he was to be John XXIII.

There was much excitement as he stood waving to what he called "an invisible crowd" from the balcony of St. Peter's. The dazzling television lights prevented him from seeing anyone as the world cheered and applauded him. He reported that he blessed the people as if he were a blind man and, turning from the crowd, became acutely aware of the responsibility he had now been given. He reminded himself that if he didn't remain a disciple of "the gentle and humble Master," he would understand nothing of "temporal realities. Then you'll be really blind," he told himself.

His first speech on Vatican radio announced the major themes of his papacy: unity in the life of the Church, including the embrace of the Orthodox Churches and peace in the secular order, particularly as the nuclear arms race, which he deplored, was accelerating at an alarming rate. He said the money spent on defense and destruction was better spent on "the least favored" in the world.

Almost from the beginning, everyone was aware that this pope was different. Now that he was pope, Roncalli was free from his vow of obedience to his superiors and didn't have to heed warnings of the decorum expected of his ecclesiastical rank. He made members of the Roman curia very uncomfortable—they were being taken places they had never trod, and almost with an added twist of John's inevitable pastoral love, the reverse was experienced by the laity. The Roman people and his staff, which included the Vatican gardeners and the Swiss guards, were made more comfortable and felt like members of his family. He stopped to talk to the common people—he even embraced them—he didn't want to be removed and kept apart. It was a freedom that came naturally to him. He made everyone feel real and was present to them as one human being to another human being. He had been perfecting and practicing this way all his life; now he could show the world exactly what it meant to be "catholic" in the true sense of the meaning—to unify and be inclusive. There was going to be much more reform ahead, but these early signs of papal collegiality and informality set the scene. It was as if Pope John had, because of his previous study of the papacy, begun to exemplify what a pope in the modern world should be. He had frequently said that the Church had only one diplomacy, the priesthood, and that the responsibility of his priesthood was to see and speak the truth, and to do so with "the utmost simplicity and tranquility," with a "radiant and serene kindness," always joyful and generous, "patient, equable, and forgetful of self," and to be loyal to God "for life and death."

THE CHAIR OF TRUTH

As a young priest working for the curia in Rome, Pope John in his journal had hailed St. Peter's as "this beautiful place of meditation and rest," praising its majestic dome rising to the heavens. He honored it as the Chair of Truth and paid fervent homage to it with his mind and heart. Now he was being crowned to sit upon it. On November 4, 1958, the feast day of his beloved St. Charles Borromeo, he was carried into St. Peter's on a portable throne by twelve footmen. It reminded him of when he would ride upon his father's shoulders as a young boy, but this time, he said it was quite windy "up there." He automatically abandoned the regular wearing of the heavy, bejeweled papal tiara, and restored some of the early, medieval costume of red velvet cape and cap with white fur border. He also dismissed the terms "the most Supreme Pontiff," "Your Holiness," and "Holy Father," which he admitted embarrassed him greatly, and instead asked to be referred to as Pope John, or just plain John. It didn't take long for plain Pope John to become "Good Pope John" to almost everyone who met him.

Pope John gave Rome further signs of what was to come during his coronation. He was not going to be a pope who sat back, remained in seclusion, and led by appearance only; he had much to share and he had little time to do it. Never before had a pope preached at his coronation Mass. Pope John stood up and delivered his homily with verve, passion, and signs of a keen intelligence, worrying many in the conservative curia who had thought they had voted in a transitional, toe-the-line pope, someone who would guide them safely through a changing period without too much trouble. Political positioning began to take hold, with its "squalid maneuvering," which tried to undermine many reforms that were to come, but Pope John was ready; he knew what he was dealing with. He once said to an American bishop that when he faced Jesus in eternity, Christ was not going to question him about how well he got along with the Roman curia, but how many souls he saved.

Two days after his coronation he met with the Italian press in a friendly, informal way. Many commented that it was like talking with a "grandfather," he made them feel so at ease. Toward the end of November, he took possession of his cathedral as bishop of Rome, the St. John Lateran (where he had been blessed with his diaconate fifty-five years before), which he said was one of the most wonderful days of his life. In his private apartment, he took to eating with his staff—Capovilla was still with him as his secretary, and eating alone with him was not something John enjoyed as he commented that Capovilla picked at his food like a canary. In a visit with John Diefenbaker, then prime minister of Canada, John commented that the realization of his solitary arrival at "the top of the heap" was on waking in bed at night with a question he wished to discuss with the pope. On remembering that he now was the pope, he turned to discussing it with Christ.

AN "AGGIORNAMENTO"

At Christmas, Pope John ventured out of the Vatican walls again to visit local hospitals and the prisoners at the Regina Coeli prison. Without a prepared speech, he spoke personally about his feelings, he embraced, he touched. The smiles and laughter captured on the faces of the men in prison, filmed for television, were enough to show the effect he had on those he met. He began getting the Vatican systems in some order and started discussing his thoughts of a Vatican Council with his closest confidantes. Capovilla was opposed to the idea of a council as he felt Pope John couldn't handle it at his advanced age, but the pope answered him that being caught in one's ego disables you from being "fully and truly free." "It's not a matter of personal feelings," he once said about Vatican II. "We are embarked on the will of the Lord."

John prepared to announce the Vatican Council to the bishops and cardinals at the Basilica of St. Paul's Outside the Walls. The renewal and reforms needed in the Church had already been drawn up with Pope Pius XII's authority early in 1949, but its obsession with "modernism" and its need for retrenchment was not what Pope John had in mind. He saw the Holy Spirit working in the signs of the times and felt himself called to lead something more expansive, an "aggiornamento," a renewal that was a radical departure from what had gone before. His announcement, followed by his request for prayers for "a good start," was received with what one cardinal described as a "devout and impressive silence." Pope John generously responded that the clergy were probably all stunned. But he was being made aware of the load he had to personally carry up "the slopes of the sacred mountain."

Even in his previous positions, Pope John had always taught that change requires patience, that all change is slow to come about, and that the course of change requires an awareness of three elements at play. He outlined these three elements when referring to the Vatican Council as (1) when the devil tries to mix up the papers, (2) when human beings help with the confusion, and (3) when the Holy Spirit clears everything up. He continued to refer to the priority of trusting the working of the Spirit within himself and throughout the community of the Church. He taught that nothing was perfect in the world and that it was necessary to "ride the storms to find the truth." He single-handedly did that during Vatican II's first stages when clearly the devil was mixing up the papers.

The changes were indeed slow in coming, even from himself. The Roman Synod in 1960 was anticipated as a practice run for the Vatican Council, but at the synod John delivered no reforms that were perceived as new. The curia responded with accusations and negative comments, which he continually referred to as "a suffering." However, he looked only for the good in all and kept his eyes fixed on the tasks at hand. He continued to publish encyclicals, including *Mater et Magistra*, an important document with a new tone in Catholic social teaching, and was kept busy with the open-door policy that he had introduced in Venice. He received anyone who wished to see him—heads of state, political leaders, royalty, religious leaders from other faiths. He welcomed the archbishop of Canterbury for the first time since the Reformation, which resulted in having Anglican representation at the Council. On one occasion, he gave his own personal breviary to a visiting Anglican priest, because he thought his looked a bit tattered. He continued to make people feel at home in his company; he guided a bishop from the traditional ritual of kissing his feet up from the floor and into a comfortable armchair to chat, and after being briefed about the right protocol toward Jacqueline Kennedy, he shocked his staff by spontaneously stretching out his arms and greeting her by her first name.

The political pressures that were gaining ground in the world during the early sixties were not something that could escape Pope John's attention. He read the reports on the ever-increasing tensions of the Cold War and the mounting missile crisis between the Soviet Union and the United States over Cuba. He dispatched a message of peace to the Conference of Non-Aligned Nations in Belgrade, and was honored by Nikita Khrushchev in the Russian newspaper *Pravda*, who said that lay Catholics should heed the pope's advice about peace negotiation over war. Pope John and Khrushchev began a correspondence, while the pope also reached out to newly elected U.S. president John F. Kennedy, who was attempting to downplay his Catholicism in the American political arena. But the pope didn't back down and drew the parties together to ensure peace. It was Khrushchev who told Norman Cousins in an interview that "what the pope has done for peace will go down in history." Pope John had said that in a nuclear age there was only one choice—dialogue or catastrophe.

The pope's seeming friendliness with Khrushchev only added fuel to his critics. Due to his "communist sympathies," he was perceived to be responsible for Italy's communist political party gaining prestige and popularity. Even as he was dying in later years, the same accusations were made of him in the press, which only added to his physical sufferings. But in preparation for the upcoming Council, he needed representatives of the whole Church present. He started dialoguing with China as well, although with little luck. Friends in Hong Kong sent him a gift of gratitude for his efforts, a small altar that he cherished and erected in his private tower in the Vatican gardens. This ninth-century tower he had renovated for prayer and solitary retreats. He called it the Torre San Giovanni (The St. John Tower), named after the original above Sotto Il Monte, of which he was so fond.

Meanwhile, he continued to appoint cardinals from all corners of the world, men from the Philippines, Japan, Mexico, and Africa, and he finally invited his first black cardinal into the Holy See, Laurean Rugambwa, archbishop of Dar-es-Salaam, Tanzania. The Church's official face was no longer made up of white Italian nobility, which worried the white Italian nobility: it was becoming obvious that there would be no turning back.

On his eightieth birthday in 1961, Pope John began feeling unwell. Many of his siblings had died of stomach cancer, and he was concerned that he would follow the same fate. He continued on his mission, however, fueled by grace, prayer, and his total surrender to the will of God. He reminded himself and others that "everything comes from God."

THE GREAT TEACHER OF LIFE

With just under a year to go until the opening of the Council, themes, programs, and agendas began to flood not only the Vatican but the public press. The more radical and liberal theologians, prominent in Germany and North America, who had been researching, writing, and teaching the elements of ecumenism already, contributed the subjects and the needs for a fresh look at theology, dogma, papal infallibility, liturgy, education, social justice, and other areas of required reform. Many, like the Swiss theologian Hans Küng, were considered to have more Protestant than Catholic leanings, but they could not be dismissed or diminished by the more conservative curia. What they were contributing was a vocabulary, a succinct interpretation of the elements that made up the reform required to facilitate change. Many were later invited to the Vatican and contributed in the sessions, largely due to Pope John's appointment of the seasoned Jesuit Augustin Bea, who was called in to oversee the planning in the preparatory commissions.

In the beginning of October 1962, when the Vatican Council was to begin, Pope John made a pilgrimage to Assisi and Loreto, two places that had touched him when he had traveled there as a young priest with Bishop Tedeschi. It seemed apt for him to pray to St. Francis for his intercession and guidance, the man who had centuries before been called by Christ to restore and renew a Church corrupted by power and greed, and lost to the needs of the poor. The first-draft documents prepared by white First World Italians did not have much, if at all, on the needs of the poor. This was to come later when the missionaries arrived with their experience of ministering to those with nothing. Addressing the needs for social action gave way to the emergence of liberation theology.

Pope John requested prayers from the whole Christian world for the Council. He spoke openly of the need for renewal, dialogue, and conversion. He said that the Council needed to reflect both St. Peter and St. Paul—Peter representing order and stability and Paul for his zeal in the missionary spread of the gospel. Bishops began pouring into Rome as never before—217 came from the United States alone and eight hundred from missionaries. There were 296 Africans, 84 from India, and 93 from the Philippines, Japan, and Indonesia.

Among the 2,500 bishops who ultimately came were those from Eastern Europe, including the young Pole Karol

Wojtyla from Krakow (the future Pope John Paul II), and members of the Russian Orthodox Church. In addition, there were ecumenical observers, translators, journalists, support staff, and secretaries—all of whom needed to be accommodated within the confines of the Vatican, which posed a physical challenge. All the hotels and houses in Rome were packed to the limit and, for the first time, St. Peter's Basilica reached capacity, filled with rows and rows of clergy, with sections erected for secretaries and staff.

Pope John's inaugural speech was a tour de force. It was the moment that summed up his entire life, all his interior preparation, all his pastoral experience, all his faith and love, and more than anything, his hope in the ways of God. He appeared youthful and manifested a sense of adventure. His main themes were the celebration of faith both old and new, the optimism of Spirit to combat the despair and gloom that was evident in the world, the intent of the Council, and the approach to dealing with errors.

He reminded everyone that history was the great teacher of life and that it was necessary not to turn a blind eye to what has happened in the past but to see how it can inform the present. He spoke of the *moment*, of becoming conscious of how the Holy Spirit was working *in the moment*, what the present age demands of the Catholic Church, and the vitalness of the education of conscience.

That evening he stood on the balcony of St. Peter's and told the crowd that he hoped to contribute to world peace, asking for their prayers, referring to the beautiful moon that shone down on them in the night sky. Then, in his usual grandfatherly style, he told everyone to go back home and give their children a kiss from Pope John.

WITH OPEN ARMS

The first sessions of Vatican II ended in December, and subsequent sessions took place regularly over the next three years, guided by Pope Paul VI. As if Pope John knew he had completed his part, he worked over the final months of his life in 1963 on his last encyclical, *Pacem in Terris*, or "Peace on Earth." He was in continuous pain, and an inoperable tumor was found in his stomach that spring. Though frail, he still appeared at his papal window and spoke and blew kisses to the crowd, who wept and prayed and stayed in vigil for him in the piazza below. All the world was struck by sadness. Here, at last, was a holy, accessible, open man as pope, and in the shortest years of any papacy (five in total) he was to be taken away. It was a slow fade. On the eve of the Feast of the Ascension on May 22, he said to the night nurse attending him (a friar from Sotto Il Monte) that he wished he could say Mass, to which the friar replied, "Your bed is your altar." His secretary, Capovilla, wept by this same bed when he heard there was no hope. Pope John turned to him and asked him to help him die "as a bishop or a pope should." In a Christlike way, he entrusted the surviving members of the Roncalli family to Capovilla's care and told him, "When this is all over, get some rest and go see your mother." His brothers and one of his sisters arrived from Sotto Il Monte, and they kept prayerful vigil by his bed.

The family and the crucifix were the last themes of his life. He told those around his bed that his entire ministry was guided by the crucifix opposite his bed, which he had seen on his waking and sleeping every day of his life since 1925. "Look at it, see it as I see it," he said. "Those open arms have been the program of my pontificate: they say that Christ died for all, for all. No one is excluded from his love, from his forgiveness."

On June 3, 1963, Pope John, the man who had embraced the world with the open arms of Christ, died into the arms of his beloved. Many called his death the most untimely of the twentieth century, yet he had completed what he had worked toward; he had come to the top of the

Sacred Mountain, what Peter Hebblethwaite called "an accurate and farsighted prophet." John had written in his journal many years before: "Certainly on the day of judgment we shall not be asked what we have read but what we have done; not how well we have spoken but how virtuously we have lived."

Angelo Roncalli's diaries were published under the title *Journal of a Soul*. Don Loris Capovilla, who was to take care of all the pope's writings and personal possessions, wrote in its introduction,

> People called him the good Pope, everyone's Pope, the parish priest of the world: he persuaded people to pray, to ponder the Gospels, to reform the morals of the world by reforming themselves. And at the end he drew everyone to be present not at a spectacle of splendid liturgical pomp but at a death bed as solemn as a Papal Mass. He ennobled death. He made people say it was a beautiful thing to die like that. The crowds who gathered in St. Peter's Square, many of them for the first time and feeling astonished at such an unexpected occurrence, looked each other in the eyes and suddenly, mysteriously, felt they were all of one family. They wondered how this had come about.

THE SECOND VATICAN COUNCIL

The Second Vatican Council threw open the doors of the Church with the twofold intention of letting the modern world, with its issues and problems and ideas, *into* the Church, and bringing the Church, with its wisdom and healing and good news, *into* the modern world.

The Church had stood apart for centuries, even resisting the changes that were affecting the world, until it was shocked by the reality of the Second World War, the Holo-caust, and the development of nuclear weapons with its added possibility of mass destruction. These events led the Church to recognize the need to reengage itself and move into the center of the questions of our age, rather than stay on the periphery where it would have little effect. Pope John XXIII had the courage to gamble: he encouraged liturgical reform and made Church teachings more accessible, even knowing he was making the Church more vulnerable to scrutiny. But he believed, in the end, that the changes were part of God's plan in contributing to the unity of humanity. John recognized that the precarious position of the divided world called for a truly ecumenical council with representa-tives from East and West. He also had the wisdom and vision to invite Lutheran and other Protestant representatives so that the Christian Churches could find a united voice.

The numerous commissions that tackled the topics for debate, discussion, and agreement originally returned with nothing new, a set of orthodox teachings, which the pope and his bishops sent back again and again until some quite progressive ideas began to emerge. The first was that the hierarchy of the Church is at the service of the people and that the people make up the Church, which led to the reform in the liturgy with celebrants facing the congrega-tion instead of being custodians to the mystery of sacra-ment. This also included the reform in language, from the historic Latin to local vernacular, and the change from medieval-inspired clerical habits to clothes of the everyday. A second progressive idea to emerge from the Council was to view the Church as a player in history, not a witness to it, removed and apart. This meant that the Church had to be involved in issues such as justice, peace, social action, and economics. Third, Church authority as it had been accepted for centuries was forced to break down and change. For instance, the structure of the Church around the primacy of the pope—the leader at the top of the pyramid with the minions of the curia all around—became more balanced between the head and the college of cardinals, enabling an important and progressive step to be taken toward reunification with other Christian Churches.

But despite these essential changes, the Second Vatican Council was called "the unfinished symphony" because it had created large movements and initiated some radical changes, but then realized that there was much more work to do in theology and lay involvement. There was more to understand, for instance, in recognizing the movement of the Holy Spirit in religious experience (and theological teaching), which was the intent of the Council itself. This spirit of renewal, of change, of embrace, would, perhaps, take generations, maybe centuries, to see it played out to its fulfillment. Steps were taken forward—and then taken back—but some permanent new movements have come from these steps. Liberation theology is one of them, the ecumenical dialogue and exchange another. The recognition of women, the laity, and the oppressed (which did not go far enough) has also become a vital contribution to the understanding of the living Church. Most Catholics recognized that there would be no turning back: some lamented the loss of traditional ceremony, while others welcomed the rush of fresh air.

Pope John XXIII always emphasized dialogue as the way to peace, a way to bring people of faith into a united whole. The dialogue that began in the first years of the Council was, in a number of cases, not acted upon, especially under the leadership of the succeeding popes. John began a challenge that pulled the rug from under the safety and security of Catholic dogmatic teaching. To this day many Catholics are either trying to replace the old rug, or are intent on weaving a much more contemporary covering, full of the vibrancy of multicolored threads.

The Church in the twenty-first century is still changing, the Holy Spirit still working at breaking up the old to make way for the new. The Catholic Church has taken a lead among furthering the cause of interfaith dialogue and embracing people of other faiths, yet forgiveness and reconciliation were necessary before any radical changes could be put in place.

The Second Vatican Council published sixteen documents of reform covering all life of the Church, including priestly sacraments, decision-making, the role of the laity, the role of the Church in the modern world, and reformation of canon law. The work continues to unfold.

THE LEGACY

Inspired by the spirit of Vatican II, John XXIII's successor, Pope Paul VI, began visiting dignitaries and the people of the Church around the world. Later, Pope John Paul II (whose chosen name reflected the influence of both popes on his pontificate) became a catalyst in liberating the Polish people and celebrated the fall of Communist Europe. It was in continuity with Vatican II that he apologized to the Jewish people and offered prayers openly at the Wailing Wall and the Jewish Holocaust Museum in Jerusalem. Pope Benedict XVI maintained this ecumenical outreach by turning toward other leaders of the Eastern Orthodox Churches and Islam.

More recently, Pope Francis exemplifies the influence of John XXIII in his style of radical openness and honesty to all. With his embrace of equality toward the poor, his love of humanity and his commitment to the practice of the gospel in his choices and manner of life, Pope Francis confidently carries forward the principles of John XXIII, who told the world that no one was less than another, that we belong to each other. Pope Francis is the first pope from outside Europe. He's a man familiar with the sufferings and strivings of all people, a man who looks beyond compliance to compassion. His commitment to ecclesial renewal and change has offered billions of Catholics the hope that all indeed can be made better. His actions and words embody dialogue: he reminds us that peace is the purpose, love is the key, and, as John XXIII asserted, Jesus is indeed the solution to every problem.

In what looked like an act of tribute, Pope Francis appointed Loris Capovilla to the College of Cardinals a few months ahead of the canonization of John XXIII.

CHRONOLOGY

1881	Born November 25 in Sotto Il Monte, Bergamo, as Angelo Giuseppe Roncalli.
1892–1900	Seminarian in Bergamo.
1900–1904	Seminarian in Rome.
1901–2	Compulsory military service.
1904	Ordained priest at the Church of Santa Maria in Monte Santo, Rome.
1905–14	Becomes private secretary to bishop of Bergamo, Msgr. Radini Tedeschi, and also professor at the Bergamo seminary.
1915–18	War ministry as medical orderly and later as army chaplain.
1918–20	Spiritual director of the Bergamo seminary. Founds student's hostel.
1921	Works at the Propagation of Faith at the Vatican.
1925	Consecrated bishop; appointed apostolic visitor to Bulgaria.
1935	Appointed Vatican envoy to Turkey and Greece.
1944	Becomes papal nuncio to France, stationed in Paris.
1953	Appointed cardinal and patriarch of Venice.
1958	Elected pope on October 28.
1962	Commencement of Vatican II.
1963	Dies June 3 in Rome.
2000	Beatified September 3.
2014	Canonized April 27.

SPIRITUAL WISDOM

"I will never recommend anything unless I can serve as an example to others...."

Saint John XXIII lived this teaching and because of his example and his writings, we can glean the essence of the virtues required for soul purification and spiritual leadership according to the way of Christ.

DISCIPLINE

The spiritual discipline and practice of self-knowledge is the training of the self and the mind to surrender, to be humble, to love, to shepherd, to obey, and to be free and in peace. Following the teachings of Thomas à Kempis, Saint John XXIII said that all these virtues can be practiced by

- Seeking to do another's will, not yours
- Choosing to have less rather than more
- Taking the inferior position, the lowest place to others
- Desiring and praying that the will of God be fulfilled in you

SPIRITUAL JOY

Through devotion to the Blessed Sacrament, Saint John discovered the experience of spiritual joy, which he said was the most important element of the spiritual life. Spiritual joy was achieved by

- Practicing courage
- Being intuitive
- Experiencing the genius of God
- Giving free rein to natural expressions of love

- Controlling the wandering mind and desirous flesh to enable the spiritual joy to flourish

LITTLE BUT WELL

During his studies, Saint John took up the mantra of "reading little, but well," and he eventually lived this "little, but well" philosophy through all aspects of his life.

DETACHMENT

This virtue Saint John referred to as the "supernatural virtue." He stated that we achieve it by

- Serenity and calmness
- Nobility of soul
- Concentrating on the higher ideals of spiritual growth and worth
- Becoming holy

HOLINESS

Holiness, he taught, was an "interior calm," an ability to smile amid the trials and crosses of life. This calm is found in the words and promises of Christ, the interior calm that is always with one. Its expression is in a "conquering charity," a feeling of renewed physical and spiritual energy, a sweetness in the soul and body.

UNITY

Saint John's passion for unity is, he said, central to the teachings of Christ, the practice of which he recommends as the basis of Christian life, "the wholehearted practice and constant practice" of unity. He asks us to consider why today's prayer and desires cannot be tomorrow's reality.

The practice of a constant interior union with God "in thought, word, and deed" is essential for understanding that part of the Lord's prayer that says, "Thy kingdom come, thy will be done." He recommends we see everything in relation to these two ideals.

In the world, the two evils that poison this thirst for and practice of unity are secularism and nationalism. Saint John prods us to aim for what unites instead of concentrating on what separates. Moved by the first pictures of our planet sent back by space, he points to the "one planet" as our home, our spiritual aim for preservation of the oneness of life. He called the world "my family."

ON LEADERSHIP AND DIPLOMACY

Saint John exemplified how the spiritual leadership and diplomacy of even one person can affect the world. The following are the vital elements he taught and practiced in portraying leadership.

- Have no expectations of being anybody except God's.
- Take on the tasks you are given, however humiliating, and do them without agitation "for goodness sake."
- Leaders must remember the problems not only of the developed world but also of the undeveloped world, including the poor, those who lament, and those with nothing.
- In all things be humble, with spiritual fervor, courteous to all, cheerful with a serenity of mind and heart.
- Show yourself by your actions, not your words.
- Avoid distractions, keep firm.
- Take the middle path in all conflict.
- Be loyal to God "for life and death."

- Be wary of honors and distinctions; they can be the "vanity of vanities." Fear flattery.
- Delegate—allow others to work and not keep everything in your own hands.
- Learn from not only the wise, but those whom you perceive as foolish.
- Free yourself from longings for change and promotions.
- Preserve "a fine simplicity" in conversation and behavior without affectation. Be afraid of saying too much on occasions, and always practice charity.
- Speak the truth and "be reprehensible in nothing."
- Remember that Christ is the solution to every problem.

SAYINGS

"The heart is the will and the spirit is the understanding. So we need a purified will and a renewed understanding."

"Simplicity contains nothing contrary to prudence, and the converse also is true. Simplicity is love: prudence is thought."

"We are not on earth as museum-keepers, but to cultivate a flourishing garden of life and to prepare a glorious future."

A PRAYER

The following two segments are taken from one of the last prayers written by Saint John XXIII at the beginning of Lent in l963.

O Lord Jesus,
Grant to the successors
    of your apostles and disciples
    and to all who call themselves
    after your Name and your Cross,
to press on with the work of spreading the Gospel
and bear witness to it in prayer,
suffering and loving obedience to your will!

May this prayer rise from every house
where people work, love, and suffer.
May the angels of heaven
gather the prayers
    of all the souls of little children,
    of generous-hearted young men and women,
    of hard-working and self-sacrificing parents,
    and of all who suffer in body and mind,
and present their prayers to God.
From him will flow down in abundance
the gifts of his heavenly joys,
of which our Apostolic Benediction
is a pledge and a reflection.

—Journal of a Soul

AFTERWORD

There was the last suffering and the death of John XXIII. In this, the Church and even the world have been through an extraordinary experience. All at once, one became aware of the immense impact this humble and good man has had. It has become clear that he has altered the religious map and even the human map of the world, simply by being who he was. He did not operate by great expositions of ideas, but by gestures and a certain personal style. He did not speak in the name of the system, of its legitimacy, of its authority, but simply in the name of the intuitions and the movement of a heart which, on the one hand, was obedient to God and, on the other, loved all people, or rather he did both these things in a single action, and in such a way again, the divine law has proved true: God alone is great; true greatness consists in being docile in the service of God in himself and in his loving plan. God raises up the humble. Blessed are the meek for they shall possess the land. Blessed are the peacemakers, they shall be called children of God. Everyone had the feeling that, in John XXIII, they had lost a father, a personal friend, someone who was thinking of and loving each one of them.

Even the incredible Roman ceremonial, those endless shows, were unable to wipe out the deep impression, the sorrow, and the intimate heartfelt affection. However, what a contradiction between the courtly pomp and that man whose funeral was the occasion of it! The working people followed his last suffering and death as though he were the father of their own family. "For once we had a good one..." A sort of extraordinary unanimity had come about.

Et nunc, reges, erudimini! [And now, kings, be instructed (Ps 2:10)]. It is clear, however, that there is a path to success because it is the path of truth: the important thing, as Lacordaire said, is not so much to leave behind something achieved, but to have a life. It is not a matter of claiming and loudly asserting that one is the Vicar of Christ, but of truly BEING it. What is really important is not so much ideas, but the heart. (Taken from *My Journal of the Council*, by Yves Congar)

BIBLIOGRAPHY

Pope John XXIII. *Journal of a Soul, 1895–1962*. Translated by Dorothy White. London: Geoffrey Chapman Ltd., 1965.

Hebblethwaite, Peter. *John XXIII: Pope of the Century*. London and New York: Continuum, 1984, 2000.

Michaels, Louis. *The Stories of Pope John XXIII: His Anecdotes & Legends*. Springfield, IL: Templegate Publishers, 2000.

Casa del Beato Papa Giovannui. Bergamo, Italy: Editrice Edinord, 2000.

Dalla Costa, John, M.Div. Contributions to Vatican II summary.